Lurch

Lurch

Poems

Don McKay

McClelland & Stewart

McClelland & Stewart and colophon are registered trademarks of
Penguin Random House Canada Limited.

Published simultaneously in the United States of America.

Library and Archives Canada Cataloguing in Publication data
is available upon request.

ISBN: 978-0-7710-5785-4
ebook ISBN: 978-0-7710-5786-1

Book design by Kate Sinclair
Cover art: Wood engraving of Passenger Pigeon © 2015, 2021 by Abigail Rorer;
The North painting by Arkhip Kuindzhi

Typeset in Aldus by M&S, Toronto
Printed in Canada

McClelland & Stewart,
a division of Penguin Random House Canada Limited,
a Penguin Random House Company
www.penguinrandomhouse.ca

2 3 4 5   25 24 23 22 21

Penguin
Random House
McCLELLAND & STEWART

For Stan Dragland

CONTENTS

IV
[Ex]

V

VI

Lurch

OISEAU TRISTE

What is the sad bird singing?
Something in the interrogative mood,
says the piano, some koan, and the violin
with the slept-in suit and smoky baritone
concurs. Outside, someone scratches
on a stone, writing out a point
or knapping in the style of *Homo habilis*, esteemed
inventor of instruments.
The five-note bird flies
in and out of opera, in
and out of flux, ferrying music
back to noise and noise,
spruced up, to a picnic in Algonquin Park.
Later, the cricket-ratchet creature.
Later, excoriating chords.
Was there a word for rock
ringing? We live between eroding raindrops
and accelerating clocks. The piano
lifts its lid to show its wire-and-hammer
heart.

I

LARIX

Larix, a.k.a. larch, a.k.a. tamarack, a.k.a. hackmatack, a.k.a. juniper

I

Soignée, scruffy; conifer, deciduous:
larch crosses categories as a smuggler
borders, accumulating aliases, bringing to staid
taxonomy the thrills of blur.
In the forest you may find one
lurking, thinly needled, waifish, lacy,
seeming spinster-frail among the bristling spruce
and trim symmetrical fir, as though
its ordinary habit was disguise. But then
autumn comes and larch goes xanthic,
goes greenish-gold, then gold, then cinnamon,
making backdrop of those steady ever greens,
its chlorophyll retreating by degrees until,
earth brown, its needles just let go.
Such ascetic ecstasy:
to renounce the juice and joy of photosynthesis
and stand there like a gibbet.
To have a mind of winter while the winter lasts.

II

Each autumn I anticipate their shift, and each
year, somehow, I'm surprised, as when a chorister
steps forward to become a star.
Isn't lyric power just
the energy of narrative withheld,

a heavy engine thrumming in the dim
penumbra? This afternoon
each needle of the larch is lit
from inside by desire and outside by the late
elegiac sun. Being spare and delicate
each enjoys an eachness not
claimed by other conifers.
Among this moment's
untold tales are girls in danger
turning into trees and trees
threading their needles with light.

III

It often comes to mind, the old tamarack, which occupies its place,
in both my mind and our woodlot, as a naturally occurring totem
pole. It seemed always to be dying and never dead, its few live
branches like defiant flags flown from an all-but-abandoned
outpost. Unlike the oaks along the fence lines, who managed time
with the ease of a Handel aria, the tamarack seemed an
accumulation of near-death experiences, gnarls becoming
re-gnarled as years became decades. Back then, in the fifties, it was
the only large tree in a field of crabapple and buckthorn, and a
constant reference point for locating picnic spots, grouse sightings,
and the like. For several summers bees nested high in its trunk.
Around it lay its lost limbs, whitening, growing harder and drier
without rotting, until they disappeared in the long grass. When I
read of the Valley of Dry Bones, it was the tamarack's fallen
members I visualized.

During the decades while the tamarack endured, the elms
were dying all around. For Glengarry County, the Dutch Elm
Disease was a catastrophe. Catastrophe? Yes: imagine Switzerland

and then subtract the Alps. The elms had been our slow fountains,
arching in effortless camber over the pastures and cemeteries,
conferring benediction on the limestone fences, the Holsteins, the
French Catholics, the Presbyterians, the Scots Catholics, the cheese
factories, the Maxville Highland Games, and the Williamstown
Fair, as well as the quaint whitewashed cabins remaining from
colonial days. Our lane still makes a distinct jog, a sidestep like a
knight's move repeated every time we approach the cabin: this
lurch is the vestige of the lane's custodial elm. After they died, the
elms loitered like oversized skeletons advertising their defection, a
disgraced clergy still hanging around the church. Those
overarching limbs turned into widow-makers, as our neighbour
Henry called them, waiting to fall and maim the man who dared
saw or chop at the trunk. Eventually they all collapsed or were
felled, leaving a series of holes in the sky, raw mouths broadcasting
the end of the pastoral tradition.

Meanwhile the tamarack persisted, year in and out, dancing its
precise tango with death, entering that bony embrace each winter
to steal its unnameable secret.

IV
Nowadays I'll come across a larch
presiding over sphagnum moss, blue flag,
and pitcher plants, the bog's thin
sinuous chanteuse. Those fine-haired tufts,
sparse and diaphanous,
could be pre-adolescent or post-chemo.
Tiny seed-cones nipple its limbs, and
if we skin the bark we find a wood
that's sister to the otter, resinous
and oily, so immune to rot it's said

a water pipe of larch will last you sixty years.
Innu people, so I've read, would pound the bark
into woundmeshing glue.
And I recall the time,
up north, being told that tamarack
was difficult to light, but could, once lit
melt the very stove we sprawled around,
with our stubby pints and smokes—rehearsing,
in the blunt argot of our kind,
the profane wonders of the wilderness.

RHIZOSPHERE

Let's pause and listen for what's happening
underground, with the roots, the rhizomes, and
their close associates, the fungi and the worms.
So much mycorrhizal promiscuity and death, such
heavy sinking and sucking among the microbes,
so little regard for personal identity and
human rights, such continuous French kissing,
the birch and the russula mushroom, the boletes
and the larch, the pink lady's slippers and their special
fungal friends, all those hyphae busy
hyphenating, dung-dirt, corpse-compost, root-rot, the great
ur-symbiosis that is soil, the ecstatic, indecent,
death-dissolving dance that will one day
gather us up.

TO SPEAK OF PATHS (2)

After we'd bushwhacked from the river up
through the blowdown from the latest hurricane,
high-stepping in our snowshoes over fallen
trunks with exaggerated wading-bird-like
care, after we'd crested the hill and kept on
getting thicketed and snarled among the
scrubby witch's hair and old man's bearded fir
we came across some tracks, dog-like, but registering
hind-to-fore, large fox or small coyote,
we couldn't say, making a wavering
uncluttered way among the trees and so
we took them as our path.
Which way is the way? A question
to be pondered and if possible
outwalked. And yet we hoped
the fox or coyote had been headed
for a little bog we knew, bordered
by a rock face, with pitcher plants and old larch
twisted and re-twisted into hieroglyphs
of hard gnarled thought. Years ago
we'd come upon it from the other side
and stopped for lunch, so if we
bushwhacked to it now we could describe
that cherished human form, The Loop,
in which each outward step we take is
taking us back home. Will people
ever tire, I wonder, of reinventing wheels?
I stepped off to one side

to see if I could glimpse our ("our")
little bog, and didn't, but as I turned back
came across a nest, chest-high,
filled with snow as though
to nurture winter. Around this little crèche
we hovered. Blue Jay? Crossbill? In the late
angled light its crystals dimmed and
quickened, quickened and dimmed within
the blunt grey twigs of its rim,
a bit like a tear, a bit
like emptiness poking its nose
into the afternoon. You took photo
upon photo, then we took our parka-heavy
perishable bodies back to the path.
There is a hope—ancient,
anthropoid—that wilderness,
despite everything, that wilderness keep something,
some souvenir of us not forced upon it,
keep something mortal and ingenious, a snowshoe print,
a sleeping place, a far-flung loop; that,
after we've gone, a fox or coyote—
we won't be choosy—come upon this path and pause
to inhale our identity ("*people,*
from this fine synthetic funk and these
comically blunt prints") before trotting on.

BIOSEMIOSIS: SOME ISSUES

Sign, sing, signify, what
are they up to? It seems
unofficial fishiness is rife, and swims
in every kind of sense unheard
by words. It seems the sleeves
of the sea are neither empty nor
indentured to *poiesis*, it seems forests
bristle with encrypted messages
we seldom intercept. Something about
making music, something about making mind
from cries, calls, hormones, flyways, mimicry,
pissmarks on trees, habits, weather, dance,
deception, warblers navigating by Earth's own
electromagnetic field, whose eerie aura radiates
from perturbations in its molten iron
core. Who knew this? Not me. Beyond the text I
take for world, they thrive upon
my absence and without my fine
hypersymbolic chat. They sing. They sign.
They signify. They mean. Were they
creatures of dream or speculative fiction we'd
be less perplexed. Were they chaos. Were they
evil. Were they drug-induced. Were they Disney. Were
they "the mindless hostility of nature," we could
resurrect grand humanistic schemes or even

Existentialism. But it seems
the butterflies and moths had simply known
("known") of the tornado long before
it huffed us and our buildings flat
and flown
                    significantly

                                        off.

SONG FOR THE SONG OF THE CEDAR WAXWINGS

Tinnitus? Or have you been
beset by angels whinging
in your belfry *sreep sreep*
sreep through the upper reaches of your ear
as though the air up there were itchy
and scratching itself. One glimpse
of their busyness among the branches
and it all comes back:
a table is being set outdoors
by a flock of aunts and in-laws, everyone
is coming and nothing,
nothing is being delicately parsed.

STANDING SNAGS

Every autumn they would die a little,
now they die a lot. They're
into it, Beethovens of decomposition,
Beatles of decay—so long, slow fountain
of transpiration, farewell mundane miracle
of photosynthesis—
                    they're into it,
dispensing their bodies in bits, undressing
in public while their limbs
gather the wherewithal to fall.
They're emigrating to the rhizosphere, whispering
non-being is the mother of being
as they feed themselves, shred by shred,
to its assiduous recyclers.

SONG FOR THE SONG OF THE ROSE-BREASTED GROSBEAK

If you hear a robin who's had voice lessons,
Roger Tory Peterson suggests, it's probably him.
OK, but not a robin who's gotten uppity, not
the pop star doing it to the anthem,
adding spangles and boosting the bombs
already bursting in air. Imagine
Ella Fitzgerald in the shower singing
"You are my sunshine," loving the notes,
but letting them swell into surprises
all their own, music with mischief in its back
pocket. While he's filling the morning with rose-
breasted ease, the missus,
perched nearby in her polybrowns,
isn't overly impressed. For her
it's the usual. Up in their nest
she'll lay three whole notes:
silent   potent   perfect.

WHITE ASH

At last the Emerald Ash Borers
have arrived in paradise, been given
an all-you-can-eat ticket to a land
where ash is plentiful and no one,
but no one, cares to eat green
gem-like bugs. Under the bark their larvae
tunnel and munch, munch
and tunnel, making trails and galleries
and leaving behind protosanskrit
scribbles. If you find
that you can read them, you'll be famous
among linguists, psychics,
and ecologists.

Affable ash,
we have cherished your straight
splits-like-a-ribbon grain, perfect
for hockey sticks, axe handles and chairs.
That suppleness in the paddle
was the medium through which
the river spoke to my wrist, my wrist
conveyed my wishes to the river.
This rocking chair, said Angus—
who made it—"come from the heart
of a big ash," its rhythm, like Angus, slightly

off-kilter. I rock and remember, remember
and rock, accompanied by companionable
creaks. Where
shall we turn for flex when you are gone?
Où sont les frênes et bullshit bricoleurs d'antan?

SONG FOR THE SONG OF THE CATBIRD

Riffs, noodles, mews, rigatonis, hey
bo diddley. Sweet, huh? Sweet sweet
sweat your ass off you
better believe it. No? Mew.
If I hear that song one more time I
love you. Yup. Really. Guess what?
Mew. Here it comes again sweet sweet I
could just puke. Hello! Bob's
your ankle. As I was saying
come off it for chrissakes. Sorry,
it's a girl! Really. Just joking, but, like,
seriously.

BETWEEN ROCK AND STONE (2)

High on the mountain's flank
we walked to Gera on the old cart road, stone
laid by stone, centuries of muscle strain
to even the way and make the footfall
just. In Gera, the only citizens left are goats
who squat in the collapsing cottages and bolt
when our shadows cross their doorways.
Most roofs have fallen, and the walls
shed their stones outward
into narrow passages or inward
onto bare flagged floors.
                              As I clamber down beside one wall
a stone comes loose in my hand.
I pause: shall I replace it
or toss it to the rubble all around?
I consider the craft, the effort,
the bravery of the weight-bearing lintels,
the broken crockery repurposed to fill cracks,
the small hearths in their corners
insisting home should happen in these raw rock hills,
and almost replace the stone.
Then I grow mindful of the limestone lump
itself—first seabed, then mountain, then wall—
with its lens of chert like an eye demanding
freedom from artifice and use.

                              Replace the stone?

Emancipate the rock?

                    Reader, I'm still here

in Gera, electric with indecision,
like a battery between its poles.
The Tourist of Gera am I called.

Decades pass:

a quick lizard darts into a crevice. Centuries:
empires fester and fall. Replace/
release. Release/
replace. On a nearby island
a dormant volcano will awake
and fill the sky with hot heavy soot
to fall on fallen Gera. Still,
like a frozen shot-putter,
its tourist holds aloft the stone or rock now
topped with tephra. Into
the late Anthropocene he persists, until,
in an ordinary winter storm, off
it slips. After that, Pied Flycatchers
will perch and foray from
his upturned hand. Newly minted
archaeologists enquire—did that hand
once hold a spear? A platter?
Was *The Tourist of Gera* really a Minoan server
bravely bearing an absence of *dolmathes*
into the future? But his true devotees,
the Anti-Ozymandians, believe the upturned palm
holds the nothing it always has,
that his gesture is simply a salute
to the mute heft of work.

II

LURCH

The full moon rose from the ocean
and an O rose in us—
some ancient emptiness,
something we'd never had but lost.

Who could explain such paradox?
The moon—reddish, immense—rose
from the ocean and the waves
broke as before, but now almost

into speech, as though not us but Homer
sat on the shore and tuned his ear.
Our wedge of rock was bare
except for blueberries and black flies

as the moon suddenly did not rise but
with a lurch we felt the Earth
turn toward this lit-up biosphereless bit
of its Archean self and—afterlurch—

realized that so it had been
all along, spinning in encircled circles with us
perched on this bald lump on the surface.
Who can sing the mystery of what actually occurs?

Moonlight swam across the waves
and stepped ashore, unfazed by flies,
naked as a blueberry, easily
enchanting every thing it touched with loss.

Who can sing such weightless *gravitas?*

III

SELECTED PROBLEMS IN TRANSLATION

Writing is always a rough translation
from wordlessness into words.

CHARLES SIMIC

PROBLEMS IN TRANSLATION #23: BACK DRAG

The waves exhaust themselves
on the beach and the water seethes back,
dragging pebbles so they click clack one
upon another. Audible entropy,
some say. God playing dice
with the universe. Infinity counting
losses, losing track, starting
over. Matthew Arnold heard it, amplified,
at Dover Beach, and sensed in its melancholy
long withdrawing roar the Sea of Faith
in full retreat. Sophocles, he recalled,
heard it on the Aegean and gave
its music to Antigone as soundtrack
for the chronic cruelty of gods.

Well, here I am, today,
walking by the Aegean with that
click clack in my ear.
North of here, on another island,
refugees fleeing from indecently smart armies
crowd already overcrowded camps. (Neither
Sophocles nor Matthew Arnold is
surprised.) And yet,
right now, May 6, 2018, on Tilos,

the back drag at my feet will not translate
as either fate or misery but
chuckles to itself—mountain
to boulder to cobble to
sand, affable and unhuman, the ancient
geologic joke I almost always
not quite but very nearly get.

It sounds like amplified bacon frying: "the birth cry of the universe," declares my cosmology professor from the TV screen. The signal has arrived in my living room after fourteen billion years of space travel and redshift, been tweaked to erase the Doppler Effect created by our Milky Way falling toward the constellation Hydra at 600 miles per second, then been boosted fifty octaves to fit into our acoustic range, printed with the lecture on a silver disc and inserted into my DVD player. Play it, my prof says, at the volume of a Pink Floyd concert, with you in the front row.

From my front-row seat on the sofa, the bacon frying has given way to the static that swallowed late-night ball games, the radio pulling in Fenway, bottom of the ninth with two out, just me, Talisker, and RCA Victor, when the play-by-play would begin to fray into a swarm of electromagnetic insects, me fiddling like a safecracker with the dial, c'mon baby, c'mon, while Fenway and its begloved galliards dissolved into hot froth (3000 degrees kelvin) at the edge of the universe.

Pause, reverse, replay: now it's an aural transcription of my father's silent wrath charging radioactive moments around the dinner table, when our ionized glances reflected off the cutlery into deep space. Paradoxically, my prof says, the Big Bang was also silent—that is, until 400,000 years elapsed and it had cooled down enough to cry its birth cry.

Obviously. This is the dawning of the age of analogous. If all of space-time was one calendar year. If it was a week. If it was a football field. A tapeworm. If all of space-time was the breadth of Canada, and the present was Cape Hardy, BC, then the Cosmic

Microwave Background would occur two footsteps onto the rock at Cape Spear, Newfoundland. If all of space-time was your extended arm, with the present at your fingertips and the Big Bang on your shoulder, and you decided to file your index fingernail, you'd eliminate the *Homo* genus in just two strokes. Nice going. Now collect the dust from that nail and sprinkle it on a Great Auk nesting on the Funk Islands around 1835: you have successfully reversed one of the most regrettable extinctions of our age.

Obviously. However, this excellent extrapolation falls, like the Milky Way falling toward Hydra at 600 miles per second, about three million light years outside the scope of this course. If you enjoyed it, you will also enjoy *Mysticism Made Easy*, which we are putting on sale exclusively for you at $79.90 US. By the way, if all of space-time were a Great Course, the Cosmic Microwave Background would occur one nanosecond into the FBI warning.

Pause, reverse, replay. Now it's the buzz of the wasp nest you stepped on while portaging around a rapids on the Gens de Terre River, an infuriated is-was-is-wasness of excited ions in the hot hot (3000 degrees kelvin, remember) plasma burning up grammar, syntax, and other clock-struck notions. Now is then is when is stinging you over and over again.

I think the moment has come for the I who is-was-were-am and will-be to press pause, get up off the sofa, and get itself a snack. If space-time were a kitchen. If it were a kettle. If it were a bowl of lightly salted popcorn.

PROBLEMS IN TRANSLATION #59: LICHENS

*Lichenologist Trevor Goward has described lichens as "fungi that have
discovered agriculture," and there is much truth to that.*
  —Irwin M. Brodo, *Lichens of North America*

*Nowadays I doubt if anyone would catch me describing lichens as
fungi that have discovered agriculture.*
  —Trevor Goward, *Twelve Readings on the Lichen Thallus*

Nothing about them fits what's preconceived,
no off-the-rack intelligence.
We have to boldly don

bewilderment, we have to kneel and peer
into the lifeform formerly known as
Fungus the Farmer, a.k.a.

Rock Tripe, a.k.a. the organism that's an
ecosystem, a.k.a. algae who
photosynthesize to feed their fungi and receive

winterized accommodation in return, a.k.a.
lichens, a.k.a. the mystery of the blessèd
incarnation of betweenity. We have to be

as pilgrims applying for visas to the
ruined garden, where the mystery
may appear as leafy, hairy,

crusty, shrubby, squamulose,
where it may resemble lettuce,
rags, maps, vomit,

rubber boot, flayed frog,
committees of golf tees, or headless wigs
haunting the woods. You have

to wonder, we say, fingering another
Frilly Ragbag, at how liberally symbiosis
puts on pelt. As though the lovers

lay sequestered in the public image
of their union, inconspicuous as crust
on rock or *outré*

as a burning bush, simple as leaves
wearing their maculae or the cephalodia which
signal a three-way with

some further cyanobacterial chum.
Such goings-on, we say. Such a
haberdasherizing of what is. As though

Metaphor herself descended, *dea ex machina*-like,
and fabulously overdressed, sending old Tenor
and Vehicle, with their antique song-

and-dance act, off to dally
in the wings. If lichens, we opine,
then there is hope for transubstantiation

and The Rapture. Late 19th-century,
"survival of the fittest" having seized the
troubled public mind, few credited fungal-

algal symbioses. But Beatrix Potter did,
and tried to sway the Linnaean Society—not
in person, since a woman wasn't welcome—

and was doubly snubbed. One hundred
years on, symbiosis in the interim
becoming recognized, Margulised, hot,

and women having become persons,
they apologized. Beatrix was dead,
though Peter Rabbit, Pigling Bland, and Mr. Tod

(of course) live on—part realistic animal,
part petticoated fantasy, the alien
aesthetics partnering each other, well

you have to wonder. We read about *Trebouxia*,
an alga too frail to survive the cold alone,
who hooks up with *Ascomycetes*,

her handyman, her helpmeet, or her pimp,
depending whom you ask (and when). Together
they propagate the North. Surely this is ripe

for prime time, Streep
and Eastwood, possibly, in many modes
and genres from low romance to high

hard-boiled. You have to wonder
at the will-to-form, the way it
burgeons without benefit of art or act

of language: the deep lust of basalt
to be hexagonal, the Blue Jay's chic
and subtle plumage—nameless, un-

accommodated in the so-called House of Being, a.k.a.
Hotel Humanity. Pull down thy vanity, as Ezra—
well-versed in this vice, but briefly

humbled into cherishing the green world
at his feet—declared. Back
on the trail we pause to check a pale

green hank hanging from a spruce,
gently tug one hair to see if there's
elastic running down its core: yes—

it's *Usnea*, the naturally occurring bungee cord,
much prized, says *Lifeforms of the Ruined Garden*,
by nesting orioles and squirrels.

PROBLEMS IN TRANSLATION #76: RIVER

It can seem to say hush hush or
hurry hurry hurry or
listen. It can rattle. It can
chortle. It can knock *sotto voce*
from the middle of a whorl like an introverted
woodpecker. It says nothing
in English, but will seem to whisper
englishenglishenglish as it lisps
across the shallows, as though calling language
back to babble and babble back
to burble and burble back to Bach's
keyboard concerto in D minor as
recorded by Glenn Gould with the
Columbia Orchestra under Leonard Bernstein
when the whole philharmonic kit
and kaboodle went skinny dipping
in polyphony.
          The translator sits
on the bridge with his feet in flux, his head
riddled with riffs. What
next? One of him composes
an alphabet of vowels. One
of him is in the kitchen
dancing with the dictionary, secretly
slipping its definitions to the blender.
One of him wishes that a fish—
say a quick brown trout—would just flip
from the unsayable river into his lap.

or mountain making & breaking, or
phusis, or earth-
energy-engine, or
orogeny:
        the writing of it writhes, erupts, re-
arranging plates and lifting
peaks (up, you Alps!) —, , , ,
, , — chanterelling
up from the mycelium to dance
with Li Po on his drunken summit and fall
as dusk with both abandon
and aplomb then non-
chalantly take up the mic
as MC^2:
        even hard rock,
        over time and under pressure, bends
        breaks, travels, though it registers as fixed
        within the selfie of your life.
                  In mine
at the moment, it happens to be April first
on the Avalon, and seriously
snowing. Spring, I notice,
cannot be coerced as it
fumbles its way north. Just
the same, I embrace my inner fool
and step outside: sideways snow
with icy pins, wind hollering *hush*
as it hustles them across the rock face

into mine. And in the midst
of all this ruckus, the trill
trill of an unseen junco (you there,
Li Po?) drilling its lust song
into the arms of the madly dancing
Balsam Fir.

IV

[EX]

REVENANT

Something out of memory walks toward us,
something that refutes
the dictionary, that won't roost
in the field guide. Something that once flew
and now must trudge. Call it grief,
trailing its wings like shabby overcoats,
like burnt flags. Call it ghost.
Call it aftermath. Call it remorse
for its ability to bite and bite
again. Call it Great Auk,
Dodo, Curlew. Call it Beothuk.
Call it every obsolete name, nothing deters
whatever it is that, epoch by epoch, walks
out of its oblivion and into our future.

In my childhood zoo
I made you play opposite the unicorn—
that pure white angel-animal,
too good for this world and destined
for sainthood in the next. You were carnal,
mud-loving, bad-tempered, stoking African
wrath inside the corrugated iron
boiler of your body. Its horn
pointed to heaven; yours were a grotesque
masterpiece of unintelligent design.
Nevertheless I liked yours best—
the disembowellers of big game b'wanas
who hunted your heads for trophies
and your feet for umbrella stands.

On my childhood zoo's advisory board
sat Tarzan, Mowgli, Grey Owl,
and Rin Tin
Tin. We endorsed all animals but rats,
yet never mentioned loss of habitat
or the trade in rhino horn
for cash. We never said *colonial*
or discussed the politics of zoos.
None of us observed how you'd
been grazing on tough siliceous grass
since the Oligocene—twenty-eight
million years before your nemesis
evolved—while Cattle Egrets

and Red-beaked Oxpeckers grazed on you,
picking parasites from your skin.
I wish one of us had whispered *symbiosis*—
little waterfall of isness, koan
that still eludes your big-brained well-armed
entrepreneurial assassins.

ORACLE

in memoriam the Passenger Pigeon

1.
What did you hear
in that troubling of air,
that thunder of wing-driven wind?

> Summer & harvest & snowtime & seedtime
> Seedtime & summer & harvest & snowtime
> Harvest & snowtime & seedtime & summer
> Snowtime & seedtime & summer & harvest:

a thousand thousand Noah's doves
drumming the promise of plenty.

2.
What did you hear
in that troubling of air,
that thunder of wing-driven wind?

> I heard nothing
> bursting into being. I heard
> the Cosmic Microwave Background
> trilling in my ear. I heard the perfect
> buzz of love.

3.
What did you hear
in that troubling of air,
that thunder of wing-driven wind?

It was a great scolding, a curse
revving the engine of remorse.
Infinities of feathers dimmed the sun
while we loaded our loquacious guns to drown
their thunder with our own.

Here in the grip of Number Six,
with its dread parade of signs
and portents, its mix of guilt and grief,
it comes as catharsis
to turn our minds to simple Number Five,
as though turning from a dear parent's drawn-out decline
to a disaster flick:
                one immense asteroid,
one blast the size of one
million Hiroshimas as it explodes
into the Yucatan and shrouds the planet
in debris. No one
saw it coming. No Cassandrasaurus
forecast destruction to her bored
fellow mega-reptiles. No dour Al Gores,
no Lovelocked Gaians. No climate
change dino-deniers sponsored by The Brothers
Koch. No one was complicit
or deliberately deaf. Even the nameless asteroid
was innocent as snow.

Before it hit, ammonites
Fibonaccied everywhere in amniotic seas.
Nanoplankton went rococo. T-Rex,
though fierce, fit its context *comme il faut*
as Texans barbecuing ribs at a rodeo.

After the impact,
it is said, an Albertosaurus in Alberta
had maybe two minutes. Perhaps her atoms
mixed with bits of the asteroid's iridium, which—
after the whole mess settled, and sixty-five million years elapsed—
fingered the perp.

Don't we all secretly adore apocalypse,
especially in movies, The Bible,
foreign cities, and the past? Pop culture
thinks so and the news
concurs. At any rate,
we must be grateful to the blessèd asteroid,
slayer of dinosaurs, facilitator
of our green and pleasant, if now pretty
iffy, biosphere.

HINDSIGHT

When the second stone
was cast, when Gatling
begat his gun, when to know
became to own—animals,
land, ideas, people;
when they piled the skulls
and posed for photographs, when
the fifth stone fell
like an asteroid, like
an Airbus, like an angel
crashing into space-time;
when the red squirrel popped
out of the stew pot and
up a pine tree in a flash, then
paused to boast and scold us in that brash
staccato and I said that's it,
let's get the little bugger and picked
up the first stone.

SONG FOR THE ESKIMO CURLEW /
CANTO PARA EL ZARAPITO BOREAL

Come back, Curlew, with your soft
interrogative whistles *qui qui qui,* come
back to your muskeg, your boreal lakes,
come back to the crowberry barrens of Labrador,
to your impossible migration down
the Atlantic, stitch north to south, eros
to anguish with your fast fierce wings beating
all the way to Patagonia,
                              vuelve, Zarapito boreal,
con tus suaves silbidos que interrogan
qui qui qui, vuelve a las pródigas playas
y pampas, vuelve al aire místico
de los Andes, hilvana el norte y el sur
el eros y la angustia, con la fuerza de tu aletear
vertiginoso, vuelve
                              bearing your fine curved beaks
as live meridians, as scimitars, as phrase marks
in the canto largo of the planet.

Observe the polished cabinets, the pedestals
awaiting your ascension, the vaulted roof
and climate-controlled atmosphere.
Here you're born again as monuments,
as statues of yourselves. Out there
you were many, *outré*,
cheap. On display you're rare
and valuable as bits of Grecian urn and saints.
Your reconfigured bones—
crates of no-longer-bated breath, spare
and vacant as haiku—
echo the architecture. We love you.
We love your tragic deaths.
Make yourselves at home here,
out of the swing of the sea
and so forth.
Under UV-free, low-lumen
lights, your feathers shall not fade
nor shall your new glass eyes grow dim.
All this so you can rest in peace and not—
god forbid—
plot grim revenge.

1.

When we dug up the grave
we found a child's bones
laid on a great swan's wing.
They had never been, we thought,
the sharpest flints in the cave,
with thick skulls evolving toward NFL
helmets. We'd applied their name
(from Neander Vale, site
of the first remains we found)
to racists, sexists, and dull
bureaucrats.
   Now we stood abashed,
trespassers on grief, thoroughly *sapiens*
with artful implements and wit.
What would it be like to be so stricken,
with few words to call on heaven, hell,
hope, grief? And what
sharp words might we, the clever cousins,
muster for the child who one

day watched a Mute Swan (wingspan:
five feet) lift from the river in two white
swipes of Paleolithic air?

2.

What manner of wreath
might honour this death?
Some wing of language
entering earth?
Wherever you've gone
may your spirit wander
wild as a swan
in the Vale of Neander.

V

WIND'S INSTRUMENTS

Some winds come to drive you crazy—
chinook, mistral—and some
to carry us home, our sails
bellied with well-being, our coffers full
of rocks to make us rich.
There is a wind for the hare,
a wind for the harrier, a wind for
lovers and another for rogues,
and one to carry scraps of racket
from as far away as Bay d'Espoir
and L'Anse Amour: *you always, I never,*
I'm out of here, fuck
off. The wind that blows
across the ice will steal the heat
from your house and creep up
from your toes until it
suckles on your heart. There is a wind
                and a wind
                and a wind for
the swilers and a wind for the seals. A sweet
breeze passes through the clarinet to make air
introspect, finding nesting cavities inside itself
for species yet unnamed. One gets
compressed in the accordion and sings
the reedy wheezing music of the river. Another

works out in your chimney, wuthering
into muscle until it finally
debuts in the bedroom as your fetch.
A wind from the Arctic,
a wind from the West,
and that sick southern
narcissistic wind that broods and feeds
upon its brooding, winding the clockwork of depression
into adolescent wrath, oh to blow down
buildings, tip up trees, to huff the forests
back to barrens, the barrens
back to bedrock, to blow the biome out
like candles on a death-day cake.
                                        And once
it's done we've had enough of wind.
We sit. We reckon the wreckage and refrain
from any form of gust. No cough.
No sneeze. No gasp. Nothing
to laugh at.
                        Until here's a little skirmish
come to ruffle your hair and lift
the fireweed fluff, to loft a pair of ravens
into aerial duet and hang plastic bags
in trees like shredded
non-biodegradable ghosts.

VI

MOTHER CAREY'S CHICKENS

a.k.a. Leach's Storm Petrels

Genetically related to shearwaters,
metaphorically to stray thoughts, lint,
lost souls, St. Peter, and
moths. Their fluttering, paddling,
dabble-the-water dance across the waves
suggests someone enraptured by a miracle
in which he does not quite believe.
                                        One
night in a lightless cove
I held one in my hands, ready
to release it to the ocean, though it seemed
too delicate to endure the crash
boom hiss of the stark North
Atlantic. Peril for us,
I told myself, home
to this weightless bit of being
in my hands. Now the lost souls
were my infant sisters on leave
from their unmarked graves.
'Why is there not nothing' was
the stray thought that returned to roost.
When they come ashore to nest
their enemies are foxes, cats, sceptics,
Black-backed Gulls and the bright
lights of the city. At sea
that dabble-the-water dance

plucks plankton from the waves.
I have read of plovers
who clean the teeth of crocodiles.
Why is there not nothing?
I watched it flutter off
in the general direction of Iceland.

SNOTTY VAR

[He] went out into the garden where there was an abundance of
balsam fir, and he brought back a strip of rind on which there were a
number of 'myrrh bladders'. He cut open the bladders and squeezed
the 'myrrh' on the cut. Of course the bleeding stopped, and within a
few days the cut had healed nicely.
   —M. Hopkins, quoted in the *Dictionary of Newfoundland English*

There is a balm in Gilead
and also in the boreal forest
where it sometimes goes by Balsam Fir
and sometimes Snotty Var.
Under its bark the myrrh
bulges into blisters—a healing balm,
a glue, a gum to chew for exercise
and medicine.
The dance of Snotty Var goes
slow slow slow slow
slow, up to eighty years or so,
then quick. Its seedlings tarry in the shade,
dormant, acting as though being shrubs was all
they ever wanted, to fur the hillsides
so they resemble massive sleeping mammals.
Then some elders fall, thanks to
heart rot or a gale (or both),
the canopy gapes
and the little firs get growing,
thickening ring by ring and climbing
rung by rung, their needles guzzling light

while their roots grope
sideways over bedrock.

Maple occupies the flag.
"Pine-clad hills"—long gone—claim
tenure in The Ode.
But it's Snotty Var that populates the woods
we can't see for the trees, closing
companionably around us, oozing snotty
wisdom—frankumsence,
turkumtine, and myrrh.

TRAIL MAINTENANCE

I know this trail like
the back of my own hand, which is to say
not all that well. Wrinkles,
liver spots, moles, the wonder of the thumb's
opposability, the missing knuckle set
like a blue note in the quick quintet—all
invisibly familiar. I know
this trail the way I know the streetscape
of a dream, there's a well-worn
shortcut that will take us to the
lecture except now it's a
cul-de-sac, ok, so we'll turn back except
now you're missing and the way's
blocked by a checkpoint *shit*
lamarde we should have hung a right
back there before that blue note, before everything
turned strange. Back when the trail
was a series of sweet unconcealings, sun-dappled,
moon-misted, when it mirrored mind,
as Emerson so cheerfully proposed.
I know this trail erases
entire episodes each time
I turn my back. The flagging tape fades
to a tan that mimics fading leaves before it falls
among them, a Kim Philby home ("home")
among his comrades ("comrades"), fitting
diligently in. Something there is that loves a trail
so truly it sends branches into it and rhizomes

under it to sprout and spread like
rumours. I know this trail
like the book I thought I knew because, well,
I wrote it, didn't I, so I should know and
somehow don't. Can you believe I called
this Basswood tree a Beech and so
my kids do to this day, having reinvented Middle
Earths while playing elves among its splayed
amiable limbs? *Ceci n'est pas un hêtre*: I plant
this sign beside that portly bole,
which will thicken up apace then
crash, a soft-core Goliath, probably
across the very trail I think I thought I knew.

Such a distance it carries,
bearing such old reptilian weight,
it arrives as a last post,
an echo of Archaeopteryx. Everyone stops
and looks up, troubled, as though
hearing a smoke alarm go off
in the Triassic. As though an ancient engine,
with its final cough, were trying to say I love you,
or possibly go fuck yourself, to its lifelong
operator. No voice from the Pleistocene
resembles this—
                            (except, well, remember
that distress call you made, part hoot,
part croak, part primal scream, when a referee's decision
went against the Pocket Rocket, and you kicked
the bottom of the coffee table, forgetting
it was not in fact a coffee table but a plank
laid across two cinder blocks, so that
a snowstorm of popcorn, plus the plank, rose
and flew into the TV set? The cry
that appalled your guests with your fandom's
Mesozoic depth?
                            Perhaps *that* voice.)

delays death. Every
dance inserts itself in flux, gathers gesture
into sense. The Bee Dance. The Waltz. Every dance
introduces grumpy entropy to eros, the native love
that lives inside our limbs trunks roots, that
flows through rapids nerves veins cambium and
makes us sexy and susceptible. The Tango.
The Cancan. Every dance picks up the mortal coil and—
watch this—does a rope trick: couples cross over,
women step out, spin, thread the needle,
run the goat. The way a living system—
Balsam Fir, for instance—winnows energy
from light and turns it into wood and needles,
resinous cones that stand erect. Paso Doble,
Hokey Pokey. Every dance
entrances time, which may slow down to Moonwalk or
accelerate to dervish with a fresh hip in its
tock. The Jitterbug. The Charleston. The Grand
Jeté. Every dance is Margaret Avison advising me
to walk in six-eight time so as to
syncopate the march. The Foxtrot. The Twist. The sweet mix
of delicate and drive that is the perfect
three-point shot. The line cast out in long relaxed
octameter that hangs above the pond to sweetly
kiss its surface. The Minuet. The Old
Soft Shoe. The direction in the Noh play that says "Dance"
and means whatever follows is: a stillness. A stagger. A lurch.
A turning wrist. Every dance resists

the current as a light bulb, a radio,
a demonstration in the square and so wakes something dormant
up. The Hora. The Highland Fling.
Every dance picks drag up in its arms,
the leap from reptile scales to feathers—
hairs that zip and unzip and negotiate
the big imperatives of gravity and wind.
The Sandhill Crane's half-lift and flap. The Dying Swan.
The Western Grebe who walks on water. Every
dance is work discovering its pulse, where
day-in day-out finds its mojo, takes that quick quick
stutter-step and pops up just in time to catch
the next log coming down the chute. The Limp. The Dumpe.
The Totentanz. Every dance makes
momentary place, the pause inside the ever-
rolling stream that fastens its attention barely
long enough to whisper watch us,
we are here, we love it, we
belong.

1.

Our eyebeams bleeding into the binoculars,
our necks uncomfortably cricked—up,
up, way up—is that microdot a pipit
at five hundred feet, a bug at one and a half, or
a speck inside my eyeball? Singing as though
the vanishing point had split
and hatched something silver:

> tiny sleigh bells (Bent), a rolling,
> jingling cascade (Sibley), profuse strains
> of unpremeditated art (Shelley), as though
> the sky itself sang (Herriot), *shring a*
> *ring a ring a* (Peterson), or

> > all of the above, all
> > of the above, all of
> > the above.

2.

But when I got to hold you
in my hand, I swore
thou wert a bird.
You occupied space.
You had weight, as the hand-held scales
confirmed. You wore
a necklace of streaks and white outer
tail feathers, cf. junco.
The field biologist took one feather
for analysis, so later we would know

at just what latitude you hatched.
In return, a tiny ring to wear
around one leg, to show how much
we cared, how much we cared where
and how, and why you will have perished.

3.
Then he said ok
let him go but when I opened up my hand
you lay there and
lay there:
>how long?
>As long as six skipped beats
>three unanswered calls
>one diagnosis.
>As long as the road from bird
>to book, from shring a ring
>to *Anthus spragueii:*
>>until at last
he nudged you and you took off up,
up, way up, so high our eyebeams bled again
into the binoculars, up where the vanishing point
splits and spills something silver into ordinary arid
prairie air.

10   "To Speak of Paths (2)":

For "To Speak of Paths (1)" see *Apparatus* (M&S, 1997).

12   "Biosemiosis: some issues":

Biosemiotics is the science of signs occurring in the natural world, outside language.

"the mindless hostility of nature": Northrop Frye, *The Bush Garden* (Anansi, 1971), p. 244.

20   "Between Rock and Stone (2)":

For "Between Rock and Stone (1)" see *Deactivated West 100* (Gaspereau Press, 2005). See also Kate Harris, *Lands of Lost Borders* (Knopf, 2018), p.141: "Geologists define stones as rocks that have been put to use. . . . At Machis [a fifth-century ruin in Georgia] I found myself wondering what happens the other way around, when our careful curations of stone ruin themselves back to rock."

Gera: an abandoned village on the Greek island of Tilos in the Aegean.

25   "Lurch":

"bit / of its Archean self": It is believed that the moon was originally a portion of Earth that detached after an asteroid impact during the Archean era.

31   "Problems in Translation #41: The Cosmic Microwave Background":

See Mark Whittle, *Cosmology: The History and Nature of Our Universe* (The Great Courses, 2008), disc 3.

33   "Problems in Translation #59: Lichens":

"Beatrix Potter did . . .": See Tom Wakeford, *Liaisons of Life* (Wiley, 2001).

Margulised: Lynn Margulis, biologist, early proponent of the importance of symbiosis.

Ezra: Ezra Pound, Canto LXXXI.

38   "Problems in Translation #82: Dragon,":

phusis (Greek): natural process.

Li Po: see "9/9, Out Drinking on Dragon Mountain," *The Selected Poems of Li Po*, trans. David Hinton (New Directions, 1996).

48   "Contemplating the K-T (Mass Extinction #5)":

K-T: the boundary between the Cretaceous (K) and Tertiary (T) periods, marking the date of the fifth major extinction following the asteroid event 65 million years ago.

iridium: a layer of this mineral, rare on Earth but common on asteroids, was found on the K-T boundary at many locations on the planet.

51   "Song for the Eskimo Curlew":

This curlew's migration extended from the high arctic to southern South America. See Fred Bodsworth, *The Last of the Curlews* (Dodd, Mead, 1955).

The Spanish translation is by Rosalind Gill.

61   "Mother Carey's Chickens":

Mother Carey: the Virgin Mary.

petrel: the name derives from St. Peter, who briefly, tentatively, walked on water (Matthew 14: 29-30), as Storm Petrels seem to do.

63   "Snotty Var":

The Ode: *The Ode to Newfoundland* begins, "When sun-rays crown thy pine-clad hills."

frankumsence, turkumtine, and myrrh: terms for fir resin in the Newfoundland dialect.

65   "Trail Maintenance":

shit lamarde: a *franglais* expression of dismay; also the name of a bicultural trickster figure.

Kim Philby: a notorious spy who operated as a mole inside British intelligence.

70   "Song for the Song of the Sprague's Pipit":

Sprague's Pipits (a.k.a. Missouri Skylarks) resemble the European skylark celebrated in Shelley's poem. They are hard to spot, since they are either singing at such a height as to be all but invisible, or hiding in the grass where they nest. Their lives on the prairies are at risk due to loss of habitat— native prairie.

"Bent": A.C. Bent, *Life Histories of North American Birds*. (Dover, 1964).

"Sibley": D.A. Sibley, *The Sibley Guide to Birds* (Knopf, 2003).

"Shelley": Percy Bysshe Shelley, "To a Skylark."

"Herriot": Trevor Herriot, *Grass, Sky, Song* (HarperCollins, 2009).

"Peterson": Roger Tory Peterson, *A Field Guide to Western Birds* (Houghton Mifflin, 1961).

ACKNOWLEDGEMENTS

Several of these poems were composed to be read at public events in The Boreal Poetry Garden in Newfoundland under the artistic direction of Marlene Creates and in collaboration with other artists and natural historians. These include "Rhizosphere," "Problems in Translation: #76 River," "Wind's Instruments," "Snotty Var," and "Every Dance."

Versions of poems in Section III were composed for the *Song of Extinction* event performed at the Luminato Festival in Toronto in 2016.

Versions of some of these poems appeared in chapbook format as *Larix* (Vallum Poetry Series #23, 2015).

Versions of "Revenant," "Curator Welcomes Relics," and "Every Dance" appeared in *Angular Unconformity* (Goose Lane, 2014), and are published here with the publisher's kind permission.

"Western Black Rhinoceros" was commissioned by Abigail Rorer of The Lone Oak Press as part of a forthcoming book of engravings and poems about extinction. That is Abigail's Passenger Pigeon engraving on the cover. Many Thanks.

"Oiseau Triste" is for Rose Bolton.

"Lurch" is for Marlene Creates.

"Problems in Translation #59: Lichens" is for Trevor Goward.

The Spanish translation for the southern hemisphere of "Song for the Eskimo Curlew/ Canto para el Zarapito boreal" was provided by Rosalind Gill. Many thanks.

"Wind's Instruments" is for Christine Carter and Florian Hoefner.

"Every Dance" is for Louise Moyes and Nicola Hawkins.

"Mother Carey's Chickens" is for Holly Hogan and Michael Crummey.

"Song for the Song of the Sprague's Pipit" is for Trevor Herriot.

Thanks to friends for helpful feedback, including Marlene Creates, Elena Johnson, Luise Hermanutz, Matthew Hollett, Anna Swanson, Tia McLennan, and Maggie Burton; to Terrence and Courtney Howell of the Grates Cove Studios for their hospitality; and to Lynette Adams for internet services. Thanks also to the patient, attentive, and nimble folks at M&S, including Kelly Joseph, Peter Norman, and Dionne Brand.

DON McKAY is the multi-award-winning author of thirteen previous books of poetry, including *Paradoxides*; *Strike/Slip*, winner of the Griffin Poetry Prize; and *Camber: Selected Poems*, a finalist for the Griffin Poetry Prize and a *Globe and Mail* Notable Book of the Year. *Angular Unconformity*, a collected poems, appeared from Goose Lane in 2014. McKay has taught poetry in universities across the country. He presently lives in St. John's, Newfoundland.